FOOTHILLS

POEMS

AND

TWO LOVE STORIES

ZOE MARIE BEL

FIRST EDITION

Designed by Winter Bel Arts

Cover art by Zoe Marie Bel

ISBN 978-2-9591921-0-4

Dépôt légal : février 2024

Visit **scatterpunk.com** to read more about all our books
and merchandise, as well as to buy them.

For my mother Maggie

CONTENTS

PART ONE

————

TRAILHEAD

It's A Love Song

Let me give you peaches. Let me reach for something
You need. Let me spell words for you that make
It seem that Yale shirt is yours indeed. Let me slosh
Through the rain with profiteroles. Let me fingertip
Your every vein. Let me rum up your Coke and
Strum something dope on this guitar when you are
In pain. Let me call it your birthday right now.
Let me hum to you and have you know somehow:

It's a love song. You are the honey in my bees.

Let me dust and gleam up your windows. Let me
Get lucky and win you a stuffed bear. Let me put
Petals in your hair for you to shake out everywhere,
Dancing in the Laundromat aisles. Let me draw
Smileys in the steam of your shower. Let me bet
I have a coupon for that. Let me confess I have
Lied, I've faked pain, I've smuggled headsets
Off planes. I am not great, but all the same:

It's a love song. You are the ocean in my breeze.

Let me plot our escape through the storm drains.
Let me take your earlobe in my lips like a grape.
Let me run at dawn from the baker so that
The bread is still warm when you wake. Let me
Aggravate dogs to amuse you, let me break ten rules
That you choose. I'll start fires, deflate tires, scale
Telephone wires, and I'll lose, oh I'll lose, for you.
I'm a wisp of might who at best is half-right but:

It's a love song. You are the devotion in my knees.

Apprentice

Line up the roads below the sun
And I shall walk them, every one,
If with those far-dusted steps I would prove
My heart from you had never moved.

Open all the books and have me absorb
Words that have from fluent hearts soared,
If with this wisdom I might then craft
Praise for you as rich as your laugh.

Share with me the way to your tears,
And I'll guard that path against cavaliers,
If in that stance I might make certain
You are never by sadness intruded again.

The tree-tips that snick the window at dawn,
I will trim them so you may dream in the warm,
If from unbroken sleep you would rise
And recognize me, the apprentice of your eyes.

Yes, let me strive and heft and smile to do these,
And tell it soft to your ear, or hard on my knees:
If there are many of me, and I'm sure that is true,
Beauty, oh beauty, there is only one of you.

Broken Umbrellas

The streets are full of broken umbrellas,
The stoplights play dead five blocks long;
The love songs tell us it's all in the stars,
The inbox favors quick loans and thongs.
The priest is wanted for child support,
The teacher can't talk about God;
The artist's got debt and a burner phone,
The star's a minor with a security squad.
The bank bought my life in the fine print,
The web knows fifty ways I'm not well;
On and on the chapels and the strip joints
Tout their exit visas from hell.

Through it all, this rent-haggard sidewalk
Offers no obvious way back to right,
But drifting with you by the burbling drains
I feel no malice in the cosmos tonight.
Amputated bicycles, embossed into railings,
Glimmer survival in the riverside cool.
I keep my eyes primed, my steps keen,
Find I am ready to be reschooled:
In the meaning of things, in the dreaming
That sings noteless in this air with you.
Look at our faces beaten in the wind,
How they're almost remembering being new.

Slouched Pepper

If you still dream of the Carolina sun and finding someone
For gas dollars and to endlessly fool the demands of today

Into tomorrow, living always like a forward slash:
Headlong, maybe falling, in a borrowed Pontiac that does

Stalling almost as well as you. If your heart is still
A broken rhythm that might be perfect with the right

Wounded song. If your dreams are mountainscapes long,
But your time left maybe not much more than this one

Drinking straw. Pick me up, *mi cielito*, I'll be under
The slouched pepper tree. Plastic shades, expired

Sunscreen, a watermelon and no knife. The Earth is
Tipping the light out of itself. Skeeters trembling

In our headlamps, we will, if you still dream, dream.
Across lines, between smokestacks, just in time.

Fields

In these dewy fields, the evening cools, and
We wait for the birdsong to end. The two of us
The champions of burned bridges, we could not
Summon one friend. There was no plan in
Pulling over, any more than in choosing to run.
Now clouds pile their bruises on the mountains,
And the corn rocks with the run of the breeze.
(Or maybe it's all those we've wronged, come
On their knees to corner us.) Should you become
The worst thing I've ever done: very well.
But the car soft-creaks as it loses heat,
While the scent of distant firs makes it through;
And I think perhaps all those ill-trodden tracks
Were my way of earning you.

Extra Leather

When I am old, let me tell you what I'm going to do:
I'm going to love unwisely, and probably you.

I'm going to get mad drunk on someone else's wine,
And demand that some young punk doggy me double-time.

I'm going to wash my car with bunched-up sexy knickers,
Weird out all the neighbors with conspiracy bumper stickers.

I'm going to let my newspapers pile up by my door,
Call it an American history museum, ten bucks to see more.

I'm returning all my kitchenware for my guaranteed refund.
When they quibble it's decades old, I'll flash them my shrunken
buns.

I'm heading mapless to New York City, and, guided only by
hunch,
I'll tell tourists local bullshit in return for three-course lunch.

I'll walk up to drive-thru windows, haggle my order real cheap,
And if they honk at my slow ass, I'll pull out some fake plastic
heat.

I'm going to get a lap dance and pay for extra leather,
And should there be conversation, I'll say: That's very clever.

On the math of it all, they keep shifting the posts;
Eighty the new seventy, it's not clear when you're toast.

So I'm calling this one early: I am formally done with youth.
From this day on let it be known I'm a cantankerous old goof.

So now that I'm officially old, here's the master plan:
I'm gonna be what I already am and simply not give a damn.

I'm going to open wide my heart, knowing it cannot be broken:
All that I've done, but here I remain, unteachable and outspoken.

Yes, I'm going to love like a goddamn fool, and probably you.
So when you're ready for cuffs and ridicule: come and be old too.

Imagineers

For another date, you'd have to quit smoking.
Those were my terms. Not just refrain awhile -
Hard quit. Destruction of all raw materials
Was just the start. I wanted a total refit
Of identity: so wholly not a smoker now
That you might never have been. No
Trailing hints in our fitting room kiss, our
Shared profiterole spoon. That was what
I'd need. At least if you wanted coffee again.

You thought about it for a week. Negotiations,
Proposed by you, took place in the DMZ
Of an old barge turned tearoom on Left Bank,
Too splintery for romance. You thanked me
For the opportunity, but explained a future
Without your Gitanes seemed Hieronymus,
As in Bosch, and you'd inevitably relapse
Then deny it with mouthwash. Your honesty
Admirable. Still, we parted wistfully and grim.

Next month, your postcard said quitting
Would less cripple your humanity if there
Were a reward. Daily. And daily changing
Because you got easily bored. A Pink Lady,
Chilled just so — that might be Monday.
Position privileges Tuesday. Wednesday,
A button from a far-gone election year.
Small things. With no ideas from you, as
Hadn't I always called myself an imagineer?

That's how I wound up scouring Texaco
Or Dairy Queen or (desperate times)
CarpetLand, en route to our rendezvous,
Your reward left to the last minute. Rules
Undiscussed but hardening over time:
No big spend, nothing alive, no aftermath.
Slight, disposable glories. To outjoy
A drug without tiring, that was the dare.
An illicit snip of purple carpet enough.

At least, that one time, and to win another day.
Our agreement holding, like our breath.

Mess Tonight

Let's make a hell of a mess tonight.
Let's confess to crimes on TV we haven't done,
Then barricade the doors like we're on the run.
Let's wear shades in bed and speak French,
Or whatever we invent that sounds like it.
Let's snort a line of Tide off the formaldehyde.
Let's howl at the moon like dogs in cartoons,
And yell, 'Fuck the government' every time a red-eye
Flies by. Let's make pancakes in the shape of
Each of the seven states between here and home.
Let's bite and tangle and knot our two bodies
In ways uncharted and not for the faint-hearted.
I am not faint of heart for you.
How about it, sugar. Make a mess with me tonight.

Let's royally screw it up tonight.
Let's prance because we lack the grace to dance.
Let's roll up tobacco in a twenty-dollar bill,
And smoke it with, 'In God we'll trust if He'll
Reveal a hundred somewhere.' Let's watch
Bread rise in the oven. Let's form a coven of two
And devise spells for those we despise.
Let's make paper planes to confuse alien ships
And throw them hard over the satellite dish.
Let's insist wrong answers at game shows,
Spit grape pips at the fake chandelier.
Let me sign you with my tongue. An autograph
From the one with whom you assailed politesse.
How about it, sugar. Make a mess with me tonight.

Let's create magnificent disorder tonight.
Let's tie together sheets to backward creep
Out the window, freight-train-bound to
Some other town. Let's write vows on
Paper towels, see if they smear or stay clear.
Let's prowl around with the lights out like thieves
And steal each other's keys so we can never
Leave. Let's declare love in voices that aren't
Ours, so that it doesn't have to be true if you
Don't want it to. Let's go very still until
Breathing and skin on skin is all that's left
To explain why we're here, defying the pain of
Tomorrow, from which I've merely borrowed you.
How about it, sugar. Make a mess with me tonight.

Not Fallen

My moments are lived like warm honey.
I walk by the lake, suddenly, brutally
Awake to my breath that freezes white
In the air, the throb of my life preserved
Right there for an instant. Before you,
Smiles were what the obedient wore, blandly
Put on, a greeting-room chore. Now each
Passing smile is glory, an overheard line
From a story that I'd like to know.
You have made me curious again, about
The hope in seasons, the sway of the glen,
This sidewalk maul of fallen leaves and
The masterpiece of colors in them.

I stand lost at a routine intersection.
Fingertips tender where I gripped coffee
Too tight, attention on you and the flickered
Amusement of your smile in the L-train light.
I'm stalling in all I once knew: unschooled
A little more with every reverie polish
Of you. Wrong season's shoes,
Only one glove – no, I'm no one's idea
Of good governance. Let them have
Their geometry of purpose, their walking
Always the circumference of emotion.
That never got me anywhere like this.

I'm not fallen, just in love.

Huddle

The air smells of cotton candy this morning.
Dollar coffee steams arctic-white in our hands.
'Cold out,' you say, and all my words go hide
In my knees. Please don't notice what you just did.
I rearrange my feet, delve for some weather wit.
A temperature zinger, a Fahrenheit quip...
Oh, forget it. 'Long time coming,' I observe
Of the absent train. Probably that's self-evident.
I'll try again. Let me hold you, would you?
You don't hear that in my silence. On we sit,
Huddled by the station parapet.

Snow's in the news, threatening apocalypse,
At least for a day or two. 'Where can we hide?'
You smile that politely. To be safe and warm,
With no reason to go outside? I definitely cannot
Think of somewhere. Nope, this is me,
Not picturing it: a hard charge at honesty,
My place or yours or anywhere with a door.
Negotiable on the door. I say, 'They salt
Real slow around here.' And that's snow dead.
You don't hear that in my silence. On we sit,
Huddled by the station parapet.

A light bloats on the skyline: the train.
An end to our solitude too. I look at your sleeve,
Float a few more unlettered words of longing
At you. Wait, you're shifting. Shit... are you
Hearing this somehow in my silence? I turn away,
Pluck at clots in my mitts. That thing at work,
That report thing, that report thing about...

I should think of that. But: 'Hey,' you say.
Hopes tangled like long-boxed fairy lights,
I say, 'Hey.' Then I see your eyes. On we sit,
Huddled by the parapet, in unbreathing surprise.

Radio

The peppermint glow of your dash radio
Is between us, this star-pillared night.
I want to steal your hands from the wheel,
Bring your mouth hard to mine, somewhere
Double with you unintruded by light.
We are in such trouble, *meine Dame*,
Hearts so far above the safety line.
So if it's alright with you, let's not pretend
We have better selves than these.
In this doom-scraper car you never drive
Very far, let's chase a red eye across
This tired land tonight. The white tips of
The ocean waves are the most brave.
To live like that, on the edge of gravity,
With you.

I reach through the glow to your dash radio,
And switch it off. Our eyes meet in
The new dark. It starts.

All That I Feel

What do I do with all that I feel for you?

Should I fold it like a lawn chair in winter?
Should I bury it under six feet of time?
Should I handcuff it, then interrogate until
It breaks down and admits to the crime?

Do I speak calmly and agree to its demands list?
Do I call security, have it tossed to the street?
When it tramps up and down the hall of my dreams,
Do I ask that it go softer with its feet?

If it weeps should I swoop in with apple sauce?
If it scribbles should I punish it with lines?
If it's late returning my heartbeat to normal,
Should this be logged just like library fines?

Were I to whisper it, what exactly would happen?
If I rumored it then tittered with the rest?
What if I sprayed it along a subway train, then
Fled east and told the officer he ran west?

Won't you please, give me please, some direction?
Pin it to my windshield or under my corkscrew.
A diagram, a treatise, or just one big dumb clue:
What do I do with all that I feel for you.

Coin-Op Laundromat Bop

So put your five quarters in, ram the crappy door, and press four.
You forgot the soap again? Yeah, just water washes fine, um, sure.
Now it's 52 minutes of rocking and frothing, and I have
something to say.
Pre-wash already done, and I've held back so long, but I just can't
today.

You see, sorry about this, but you're really kind of delicious these
days.
Your sleepy lashes, your faded plaids, your mind-blowing,
knee-baring frays.
Time waits for no one, Tide drains away too, so here is what I
propose:
As the turbo drum spins, we let possibility in, and totally forget
about clothes.

(Chorus)
Let's eat a whole pie with improvised forks.
Let's leap on the ironing boards and surf-dance like dorks.
Let's sock-puppet "Whore" at the fluff-n-fold attendant.
Why? I don't know. Because together we're transcendent.

All these times I've changed your dimes and lent you mine
When you've had no softener. All these nights we've passed
The time with talk of coming oftener. Are my words
Getting through, above the machine's final spew?

The slow, certain ruin of multiple washes
Can't touch the colors I've found:
The ones I feel inside my heart
Whenever you're around.

No baskets left, so together we heft your sodden duds into the
dryer.
You opt for Delicates and again I explain that towels need a little
higher.
You check the lint vent - unprompted! Maybe you have potential
at this.
We hunker down, dryer thrashing around, and now... how about
a kiss.

Did I just say that? I guess I did. So now it's there, like your
underwear,
Snagged up against the dryer lid. Where does this go now, where
do I stare?
The spinner shriek's rising as my heart is capsizing at Suds'n Go
Laundromat.
But then you take my hand and - can it be? - you say it right on
back.

(Chorus)
Yes, let's eat a whole pie with improvised forks.
Let's leap on the ironing boards and surf-dance like dorks.
Let's sock-puppet "Whore" at the fluff-n-fold attendant.
Why? Well, why not, when together we're transcendent.

All these times you've changed my dimes and lent me yours
When I've had no softener. All these nights we've done
Just fine killing time with banter and vodka. Are you
Hearing me somehow as this machine has a cow?

Because the slow, certain ruin of multiple washes
Can't touch the colors I've found:
The ones I feel inside my heart
Whenever you're around.

Nougat: A Love Story

The caramel nougat in the candy box
Didn't know what to do.
There she was, five squares away,
A truffle so voluptuous and true.
Such full-bodied cocoa! Such intricate swirls!
Delicately freckled with mandarin peel!
How to behold her and then do a thing
But feel for her, feel for her, feel?

Nougat sighed, "I have no raspberry cream nor
Tender praline – how can I hope to enchant her?"
"Oh, give it a rest," snapped a raisin rum fudge,
Whose liquor streak made her kind of a downer.
"Didn't you hear about the apricot crunch
Who pined for a dewberry fondant?
Apricot sat melting while dewberry remained
As oblivious as he was despondent."

"But," said Nougat, "Did apricot speak?
Of her loveliness, of his unquenchable flame?"
She huffed, "An apricot crunch, so common
A thing, address her with her French-sounding name?
Of course not, you lump! You're a white-trash pick,
A cheap sugar hit - sad story, whatever, boo hoo.
If it comes handcrafted and is hard to pronounce,
That's booty that just ain't for you."

Nougat was silent, gave a tolerant smile,
As from raisin rum's crew there came laughter.
Such dreams in this chew, it was clear to
The rest, could only end in disaster.

But inside Nougat a determination formed,
As hard as a Brazil nut itself:
To be stronger, wiser, whatever it took;
To be measured by more than one's wealth.

And so, as the candy was opened for Christmas,
And others around them were eaten,
Nougat read up on high-confectionery ways
And endeavored by all means to sweeten.
Until he and Truffle were the only two left
(Plus a marzipan spit out, despised);
Terrified that she'd be the one taken next,
Nougat worked hard for her eyes.

Truffle, humming Bizet, glanced over at last:
"What's up, Noogs, you seem antsy today."
"No longer," Nougat cried, "Am I the candy of choice
For the gas station purchase on Mother's Day!
Now ballads I can sing, and in soaring verse string
Sentiments as sweet-crafted as you!
With these changes in me — you're seeing them, right? —
To your beauty I am paying my dues."

Truffle blinked and seemed quite enthralled,
So on Nougat went, like a butterfly set free.
"Yes, adieu to the nothing clump I once was,
Risen from gunk to smooth gallantry!
From muzak to Mozart, peep show to Picasso -
And I'll have you know I can spell 'epitome'.
(I learned that word for all that you are,
For the stairway to glory you have shown me.)"

Truffle frowned. "But your peanut lumps,
Your sticky bits. And, darling, your rickety sprinkles.
And let's not forget those dents in your coat
That look to me a little like dimples."
"Enough!" Nougat pleaded. "No more of that!
For your pleasure I am now reborn. I will melt,
I will toil, I'll steal Godiva gold foil —
And die content in the full love I've felt."

Truffle smiled a bit. "You silly prick.
I liked you much better before."

Booty Call

Fuck work and hitting sales targets and submitting for review
Reports on phase two, and nodding 'Loud and clear' to
The boss you'd like to smear between your teeth like dental floss.
Fuck the halogens in medicated white and the color patches
Like broken kites on the carpets. Fuck the Community Values
Suggestions box and the brand-aggrandizing timezone clocks.
Fuck your latte clinging, and your ting-tinging phone that
Promises you you're never alone, and your apps, time trackers,
Efficiency maps. Fuck calling all that the American Dream,
Because in fact you're stumping the line in someone else's
Prospects mine: a go-getter, alright, just not of better
For yourself. Fuck it, and come instead to my door.
I'll make your heart a different kind of sore.

Fuck gridlock and nudging your fender ever closer to the
Tender parts of the next car along, like sniffing dogs, or
Stiffening cogs in a machine that makes only ulcers and
Smog. Fuck the classes in human dumb you slavishly attend
On Route 101, where billboards tell how wrong you are
Without a new car or sitting so far from some flick about
Patriots measuring dick with the enemy. Fuck the fire truck
That always looms just as you're in luck at the light.
Fuck the garbage they refused to take because it wasn't
Pailed right, and now a racoon's raked it all over your
Driveway. You're standing ankle-deep in fail, honey.
So fuck it, and come express to this bed.
I'll take you places where no stoplight is red.

Fuck quinoa and lean cuts and pine nuts and whatever else
Is now recommended to keep your life extended, so
You can sit crooked and basted in all your mistakes and
Watch your friends expire and your kids turn out to be liars.

Fuck cable TV and its race against time to find the slasher
Or the bomb or The One, plus the ads for Senators told by
God to run for the job. Fuck your Belgian couch and your
Scandinavian throw and your smoothie maker that could cream
All the fruit in Jamaica without a sound and no bits left
unground.
Fuck your bedside book about Jefferson that you'll never
Look at again. Fuck it all good and hard, and come
Do the same to me. Because the paperwork might
Call it living, baby, but really you're dying politely.

PART TWO

OVERLOOK

Grand Witness

We have dipped our oars for so long, my beloved.
Give me your hands that have brought us here.
The work patterned in them; the tenderness
They've pressed when I thought warmth had left.
Give me your tiptoe smile, suddenly there though
You've been plotting it awhile. All the seasons
Behind us, I feel them in my skin tonight.
The harvests, the windstorms, the bobby socks
Of spring. We've seen everything. We've been
Royals on rooftops below dollar-store string lights,
Night-danced in silence to the muffled thrum
Of all that we've done and might. Our sharpest truths
Imparted in moments so slight that nowhere else
Did they even catch the light. Yes, I am
The grand witness of you, and you the great
Chronicler of me. So give me your hands,
Your smile, and, for these words now, come here.

Beloved, oh beloved, my beloved, the city glass
You unlooking pass will not tell you so,
But you walk with my love in your atoms
Surely as what burns is attended by glow.

For Jaimie and Richard on their anniversary

Salad Plans

Well, your feet are up on the table again,
And our salad plans have become Cap'n Crunch
And dark rum, downed in the gloat of the TV.
As screen gunfire zings, our cracked windows
Let in the backstreet blues of yarded dogs,
Cheated drunks, should-be millionaires.
Your hair is a mess, and this ain't no
Beauty queen's dress on these shoulders
That have gotten older pressed to yours.
Fairy tales won't grow here, it's true.
No four-leaf clovers or velvet all over
The future as it looks here with you.
Still, we've music and plates, and no plans
To escape, and with my whole heart I sing:
It'll do.

All That Said

Honey? It's my turn to talk.

Look at all our hangers, but still you toss off
Your clothes, then pay through the nose for
Midnight dry-cleaning or a new thing to throw.
You say 'Showdown city' and 'These margins
Ain't pretty' like a Wall Street mogul. Darling,
You're in graphic design! Nobody's 'going global'.

Always sounding your vowels and talking waffle-weave
Towels when your mother calls. Meanwhile slupping
Mac and cheese with no cutlery, and playing
Bondage tease with the phone cord on me.
The Magna Carta is not the wagon the English
Arrived in. 'Huh' is not acceptable in Scrabble.

And dammit, lady, you are ticklish, no matter
How much you downplay it on your face.
Name me one other person who's gotten a scar
From a piñata, or who refrigerates her mascara,
Or loses her lunch bag in her own damn car,
Or so fiercely believes she can name every star.

All that said, why don't you forget about storming out
And come back to bed. You're a whole lot of things.
I want every one of them here on my shoulder,
Sleeping it off as we get another day older. Until
Morning brings the garbage trucks yawning and
The cornmeal of first light on the walls. That's when

I'll hold you - those places. I'll murmur, 'See?'
We're a perfect mess in undaunted harmony.

Cranes

Smoke stacks talk back to the summer skies,
Grumbling sulfur, and another face from
The yearbook dies, with a lawsuit pending
And well-wishers sending emojis to the
Left-behind. Meal-replacement shakes will
Make everything better, at least according
To the teenage trendsetters on the (Times Square
Everywhere now) screens. So many screens,
All asking for money. But it's the vagrants
Asking the same that we look at funny.
College grads are put on hold, waiting to be
Told if minimum repayment will spare any rent,
While reality stars buy lenience from the city.
Safety handrails and convenience racks and
Throbbing, emoting GPS maps, and notifications
Of clicks from friends, or dead-ends ahead, or
A system update, version 2 point 1 point 4 point 6,
And how it will fix security flaws you never knew
Were there. Terror, the word du jour, they scowl it now
From every doorway: *terror, terrored, terroring,*
The art of letting fear fill everything in. Still,
The child on the bus pauses thumbs on his
High-definition Special Ops guns, and sits,
Tickled by forces he cannot name, as the skyline
Hints a drifting bird and the ocean winks
Between regeneration cranes, and
Impossibly he remembers this might be where
We're going, but it is not where we began.

Wet Paint

It's not your Snow White type, this mouth.
It has lied tall and wide, and forced this heart
To go on the run from all it has falsely won.
It has cursed the God in which it never believed,
Except when to plead for extra time or more buck
Or better luck, in return for lifelong penitence
That lasts exactly three shots and one tugging
Glance at the bar. No, these lips are far, far
From as good as new. But standing here
In the tickle of your breath, they have nothing
Left to lie about: whatever I am right now,
It's all true. The moon pastes its doubts to
The city edges; life will undo us, but not yet.
I'd get on my knees in wet paint for you.

Bring Your Noise

The way may be storm-whipped, the safety line
Frayed, and long midnights of the mind imply
You should have stayed among the tiptoers
Of their days, the doubt sowers who say:
Better that your soul not shout, accept
The clout you've been given, keep to the
Designated doors from one day to the next.
This infinite business of acquiesce,
Of pressing at life only with the force
Advised in others' eyes, is an easy disease.

Choose the harder release. Hear their unease
Merely as agitated leaves, and you
Are the breeze, beyond their harm;
Do not dignify what signifies nothing.
Think only of the future you breathe,
The letters that need you to carry them
To the stone, where you will chisel them
Home. Go beyond the vines, break a canopy
And drag in sun where the consensus is
There can be none.

To those untouched vats of silence,
Those tombs of dreams undone by fear
Before they were even begun:
Lady, bring your noise.

Walk

For A Friend In Despair

Walk toward the rumors of light,
Walk the long path of stone;
Walk though your ankles are furious,
And you could not be further from home.

Walk until the lakes have replenished
And the salesmen have run out of lies;
Walk out the poverty riot of your heart
Below the whims of anonymous skies.

Walk, walk until you feel nameless,
A no one, a soul weathered bare;
Walk, then turn, and see at that distance:
Your troubles so small now, under the air.

Home (Thanksgiving Eve)

Sunset's at the edge of town, the frost fresh-minted white;
The way ahead is written in the porchlamp pools of light.
By the fever stream of homebound headlamps, billboards
Flicker dreams; coffee and falafel fuel the living in between.

Dropped mittens and fugitive newspapers riding on the breeze:
The relics of the other souls who've walked below these eaves.
Kitchens anonymously tease out smells, promote the feast to
come,
Pigeons crowd a failed pie as the oven firms another one.

Unpaid bills or a betrayed heart might be weighing on my steps,
But something in simply walking this way permits me to forget.
Ahead, a little time to reject sorrow and dare to feel fine,
Turning from the workaday to this bedrock place of mine.

Tonight the porchlamp pools of white, they lead me on to
The opposite of alone. They write it there in tender worn light:

Home.

You Are

Faithful as shadow, giving as the sun.
Strawberry fields of intimacies, where
In gridlock my reveries run. The soother
Of lost keys. The patches on my fallen
Knees. The word I use to cheat in
Scrabble (I claim I heard it overseas).
A vast organization, the Periodic Table
Of life's best things. The notes that
Honey-drunk bees are endeavoring
To sing. The punctuation of my minutes,
The grammar of my days. The map I always
Reach for when doubt installs its haze.
The length and the breadth; the astronomy
And the sky. The presence in my solitude,
The hope whose snowcap stands high.
You are the constellation of all I thought
I could not find in one: my freedom,
My limits, my beginning, my belong.

For Patty and Warren on their anniversary

Dublin Bay (1956)

Twelve years gone, since I last stepped off this tram
And glimpsed the woman I am in the flanks of
The faded milk cans. The copper fray of the sun,
And my shadow stretched along, as though scraping
For somewhere to hold on. The sucking mud lanes
Where our smidge of a boy would hoppingly flee
With the dog-violets he'd freed from garden
Captivity. The seamstress dens in whose
Propped doors old schoolfriends would lean out,
For cross-street fuss over stockings and
Ferry fare. The shriek to the nose of piled fish
That didn't deter our waterfront kiss in which
I first felt the pressed rhythms of longing.

Twelve years gone, since I last chanced this bench,
Its limbs aslant, all its strength spent
On lovers breathing hope from its view.
They carried you home in the flag, and courage
Was said twice as many times as dead.
Our boy slept below a map, with Arnhem
Colored in black: fierce instruction to his dreams,
To go there, your final place. When the end
Of war was called, and the broken emerged
Appalled at the notion life could now resume,
I left the city, took us south, no longer trusting
My soul would not bleed from my mouth
At the tints of you here.

Twelve years gone, and all along it was our son
Who nudged your absence toward the untrue:
His heaped curls, his feet angled out
At the world as though to measure it.

At seventeen, he won a Killarney girl with
A borrowed line about the tyranny of beauty.
He's quiet now, since she made it true.
Yes, you are the architect of both our
Hearts, his and mine. Across the canal,
A trumpet sounds: jazz in the Antique Quarter,
They'll never take that from this town.
But you were taken, *a rúnsearc*, and here
I feel it, twelve years long: it is with you
That this daughter of Dublin belongs.

Foothills Of The Infinite

There must be a place, some kind of place,
Where only we can go. A bed, a few books,
The soft shouldering of a brook whose allegro
Is the sole reminder of time. A jagged fringe
Of snow will occasionally show in our
Windows framing unkempt solitude.
In the tiptoe of light across our floorboards
Toward the night, I'll fill my eyes with you,
Touch my everything to yours. We'll tell
Stories true or tall, or make no sound at all,
Simply breathe our shared air, here in these,
The foothills of the infinite. Yes, there
Must be somewhere, some place out there,
Where to live with instinct would not ruin
Us two. Where I'll hold you to my chest,
And there you'll hear it best: that
The rhythm of my being answers to you.

The Harvesters

We're looking down the length of summer.
The power lines are humming and there's
Thirsty bougainvillea in the air. We know
A little that we'll never have this day
Again, but we are sleepy and spoiled,
Maybe ruined: the low-hanging
Feelgood of sugar and plastic, the
Holographic embrace of our screens.
So we do not feel it, this finite.
We watch the minutes pale the fields
As though we are not the harvesters.

These easy breaths of ours. Think of
The words they could bring into sound.
I could say: yours is the face.
You could say: let's leave this road,
The map too, and follow the string lights
Of orchards through town after town,
Past cobwebbed barnyards glinting dew,
Pursued by the sins of dive-bar hymns.
We could leave it, you know – everything.

But there are thoughts on your brow,
And a plaintive song I used to know
Is wind-teased from a trucker's radio.
So on it goes, this safely indefinite thrum
Of us. Dollars handed between schemes
Down below, and the unseen freeway flow
Implied by a news chopper banking low.
It weighs softly, our tenderness:
Of weakly and strongly just letting it go.

Care

Dalton met Lucy on the median of a Chicago boulevard, with an aggressive winter thawing around them. Both were in their late teens, but feeling older. Dalton had his hood up for warmth and his pockets bulging with tangerines, his standard gift for the kids who hung out in the projects stairway. Lucy was under-dressed and looking to her cigarette to solve the cold, the train she was about to miss, everything.

Both had jaywalked to the median without risk. Now three lanes of traffic slashed between them and the other sidewalk, with no gaps opening up for very long. It took Dalton a little while to realize he was not alone, absurdly stranded on the median like this. As he looked across and cautiously took in the girl alongside him, he got an impression of everything he would come to know well. Beauty, such beauty, that she seemed to want to throw away. The eyes she kept tauntingly hollow of feeling. The hands that touched nothing with reverence. The overcomplicated hair, and clothes that looked mismatched and borrowed although they were hers. Overall she seemed to be poised for destruction; not seeking it exactly, but if it found her, she would not resist.

Dalton had no business sparking to such a soul.

All the same, he nodded hello. Lucy smiled knowingly, her default smile, and swore at cars. She had to catch her train, she yelled, she had to. Dalton wouldn't understand her strange intensity until weeks later, when she'd tell him her heart had just been broken, and the horizon felt like it was folding in, and the only anesthetic that worked for her was motion, furious, blind motion; that had been true her whole life. At the time, Dalton understood only that Lucy's eyes were narrowing at a gap between cars. He realized she was going to chance it. It was a suicide move. Dalton told her so.

Lucy smiled. If Dalton could do better, she said, he should take the lead. Otherwise, he should butt out. Their eyes met, and he saw that she was serious. She ran this roulette herself, or he did it with her.

Dalton stared at traffic harder than ever before in his life. Sometimes you feel life fizzing on the tip of your tongue, and you realize you are not your plans and habits, you are your instincts in moments like this.

When something like a gap appeared between vehicles, Dalton touched Lucy's elbow and barely heard himself over his own heartbeat.

He said, "Go."

And so, their friendship began.

Dalton was determined to be the first in his family to go to college. Lucy had recently decided the life of an artist was for her instead. Dalton kept his cash neatly clipped in his closest pocket. Lucy would find clenched-up twenties in her purse and realize she'd accidentally used them to dispose of her gum. Dalton had one parent on disability, the other in multiple law-enforcement databases. Lucy's family were professionals as stiff and glossy as the tennis racquets they donated to inner-city community programs.

And yet, and yet. If you can explain something, it becomes unbeautiful. Lucy said that once, and Dalton never forgot it. There was no science to their survival on the boulevard that day. There was no science to the two of them ever since.

Lucy came regularly to the West Side, where she rented a warehouse unit from a live-work art collective whose 'live' part she skipped. As an artist she was still exploring identities, with her favorite view of herself being: a curator of urban found objects. She toured the city's curb alerts, yard sales, aggressive sidewalks and industrial dumpsters for philosophically convenient artifacts such as dented mannequins, charred couches, bullet casings and wildly unspooling video tapes whose content she would 'reimagine' in Super 8 then project onto a wall behind a piled-up snarl of the tape.

Her painstaking arrangements of these objects were commentaries on modern life, she said, without really looking at him. She had exhibited in both a mall and a synagogue, a combination that was apparently enough to qualify her as an "upcoming Chicago artist" in local TV news. Lucy reported that status to Dalton with a thin smile, when he would nod carefully, and that was that. An artist, very well. Even if they both knew she missed the veneration she had once felt for that word before she had made it that easy.

Whenever Lucy was West Side, she and Dalton would meet at a blowhard Turkish diner a few blocks from the public library where he studied. The diner was popular with Canadian truckers and raggedy, fatherless families waiting for the Greyhound. Lucy would celebrate it as a "real kinda place", while Dalton sat silently cursing the gusty swing-door.

Picking at the fraying tablecloth in the casual way she destroyed things, and endlessly realigning her cocked sunglasses, Lucy did most of the talking. (Dalton was an eyebrows guy – said it up there best – and she got to know his full repertoire well.) Dalton quickly realized that Lucy confiding in you meant nothing – the facts of her own life were as worthless to her as loose change. The one-night stands she'd verbally scratch out of herself the next morning. The drugs that "reopened possibilities" for a few hours, then left her numb for days, eyes thick with misgivings and stale mascara. The way she realized she was in love with a guy only after she'd moved on to the next one.

Dalton listened to Lucy speak of her love for other men with a soft, panging horror he had no name or plan for. Whatever it was, as one day became another, and the happiness he otherwise felt with Lucy laid down stronger roots around and through that feeling, he found he could live with it.

And so, as Lucy sat in nostalgic, tortured recognition that she loved someone lost, Dalton would pour Sweet'n Lo onto her hand – a dumb, ticklish thing they did now and then. He'd smile gently and say: "There you go again. Letting the rear-view upset you."

"Hmmm, I know." Lucy chewed the ice from her soda, tipping the sweetener from one hand to the other, back and forth, until it was all spilled. "That's the only time shit makes sense to me. When it's not around anymore."

Dalton nodded, and said he expected that was true of most people. What he didn't say was that he wanted so much more for her than that. He wished he could give it to her, in fact: a right now that made sense to her, whose joy was in itself, not in contemplating the back then or the someone else she might be tomorrow.

Dalton went to Illinois State for pre-med, and met a girl there who took as natural the soft edges he'd so carefully learned. Until one day, with that girl on his arm, they truly felt like his. Lucy meanwhile went on with the same-old new, throwing her heart out in one creative direction after another, remaining an "upcoming Chicago artist" year upon year. Her experiments in wood burning unexpectedly took off, with the historical maps of Chicago she burned onto oak panels becoming must-have wall art in business centers around the city.

She and Dalton continued to meet whenever they could, in all the old places to which Dalton pretended he'd never belonged and Lucy that she always had. With others, their childhood dreams felt like fading laundry, but together they strung them up in full colors. It was easier to believe in the unlikely when your friend and you are exactly that.

Once, Dalton had written CARE with his fingertip on Lucy's shoulder, when she was absently lounging against him on the L train. That word had felt like the best abbreviation of the longer sentence he'd have written if he could. Lucy had smiled knowingly, and returned to listing the childhood rivals she now recognized as deep influences on her development.

Waving her off into the milky dusk of the Riverwalk one night, Dalton knew if this was love, it was too fundamental to him to be tested. So he'd do nothing but feel it. The most he hoped for was that, for a few years yet, Lucy would look to him sooner than cross the traffic alone.

Dogs Of Summer

It began when Denny just couldn't take the barking anymore.

It was a fierce New Orleans summer, one of the hottest on record. Kids were breaking into country clubs for soccer around the sprinklers, because only under the spray was play bearable. Convenience stores had to find inventive ways of racking magazines to stop them fluttering amid the madly spinning fans. Soda brands were advertising on everything but 911 calls.

Denny had sold insurance his whole life, then lost his wife to cancer just months into his retirement. If there was irony there, he tried not to dwell on it. There were offers of spare rooms from his children, but Denny decided to stay put in the creole cottage he and Maura had built in the Marigny neighborhood. Honey and pistachio paint scheme. A yard that crammed itself with life and color without any real effort from him. Only the occasional police chopper.

Denny would sit out on his deck and read a great deal. Classic titles the library marked for the high school curriculum, and high schoolers in turn marked with optimistic dick drawings and slurs about classmates. He'd plink at his piano, wishing he'd kept up the lessons. He'd drive to the mall, and marvel at all the new things they'd invented so folks would gain weight or lose it, and make friends or avoid them. Fat and friends seemed to be the twin contours of modern life. Short on both, Denny felt all the more that he didn't belong in this world. He had departed with Maura. What remained of him here was merely luggage and would follow her soon.

With such a view of yourself, you are not easily annoyed. But his neighbor, oh his neighbor, she could do it.

Her house was not so much a home as a to-do list writ large. Its windows were boarded up lopsidedly. Its screen door was an open mass grave for flies. The laundry strung up in her yard had been there, by Denny's calculation, for six months. Denny would have called her in dead, had it not been for the smoke that drifted up from behind the laundry every couple hours. She was out in her yard, smoking.

Denny knew from neighborhood gossip that she was around his age and had never married. At certain times of day, the sun cast her silhouette on the mildewed bed sheets obscuring her. Hers was a proud head with a crooked perm. She smoked with an odd grace: ballroom sweeps of her arm with the cigarette, then a saxophonist throw-back of her head with each puff.

She might almost have intrigued Denny, had it not been for her dog. Day and night, it barked and howled, full of sorrow. Denny knew just enough about dogs to suspect melodrama.

One night, the dog's howling wove itself into Denny's sleep and he dreamed it was the sound of the ambulance that had carried his wife to the hospital. That was the final straw.

The next morning, Denny braved the bird droppings all over his neighbor's porch and knocked on her door. It appeared that knocking was an unusual occurrence here, as a digit of her house number fell off. Denny was eyeing it sheepishly, plotting a quick fix, when there she was, beyond the screen door.

She was a large woman, most of it on her hips. She was wearing a tribal kaftan and riding boots, which gave the impression she keenly wished you to know she was not from around here. Her cinnamon eyes were impatiently curious. Nothing about her was shy.

Denny was shy, though, to his great surprise. He flubbed a few words in his greeting, then lurched into his polite but firm request: could she please *contain* her dog's barking.

Contain, Denny had decided, was the action to emphasize in his approach. He would not ask her to silence her dog, as that required cooperation from another species, and, as lazy as this woman seemed, she would quickly resort to that excuse. But contain she could do herself, with little effort, by keeping the damn thing indoors.

Yes, Denny had intricately thought it through. Everything except the woman slowly leaning into the light then croaking, "Ain't no dog a mine."

She hadn't owned a dog for thirty-seven years, since she'd saved up for a one-way ticket to Hollywood by living on construction sites. Back then, a mutt was her security. She'd heard the dog, of course, and assumed it was Denny's. It didn't bother her. Barking added character to a neighborhood, like freight trains clanking or that hippy kid scraping at his violin a few doors down.

"But it's all the time," Denny insisted. "And it's angry."

The woman thought about that. "Well, you know the cure for anger."

"What's that?"

"A heart attack."

As Denny processed that, the woman smiled and opened her door a fraction wider.

She said, "How about coffee and mayo cake while you figure out if I'm kidding."

Mayo cake was, like many things in her house, her own invention.

Her name was Genoveve. She'd been a lot of things: actress, voice coach, positivity consultant, fluff 'n' fold attendant. She'd never married because, in her 20s and 30s, there'd been so many men – all of them ripe, or a pleasure to help get there. Then, all of a sudden, those men had gotten married, a state in which, as far as Genoveve saw, "the male in a man don't exactly blossom". There had been affairs – dramatic because ultimately disposable – and there had been traveling. Mainly in hot, earthy places like Egypt and India, where eating, sleeping and fucking are luxuries. When something is luxurious, it is revered and ultimately done better ("Think about it: they got the Kama Sutra; we got Best Buy weekly ads").

A lawyer had met Genoveve after what turned out to be her last ever flight. She'd left an impression on at least one of the men from her youth, as he'd bequeathed this old dump to her. Genoveve decided to settle down, which meant to opt out of the Stairmaster of modern life. No housework. No watching her weight. No forking out for some convenience gadget that would wait just long enough for her to develop a dependency, then demand she upgrade to a more expensive model.

She didn't see her life as over. She saw it as only just beginning. It is in acting wholly for pleasure, without regard for consequence, that you truly live.

So here she was, truly living. Sprawling out her unshaven legs on an erratic deckchair, surrounded by browning grass and spit watermelon pips, smoking her ass off.

Genoveve told Denny all of this that first day out in her yard, all at once. Sensing that he had not absorbed very much of it, she invited him back the next day, and told him all at once, out in the yard, all over again.

They repeated this for many afternoons afterward, with Genoveve periodically spraying Cool Whip into both their hands for refreshment. (She didn't do plates or silverware any more than she did laundry. Denny learned to bring his own wet wipes.)

Denny was no big talker. A long marriage had taught him the value of listening, and, even more so, the hazards of an unconsidered remark. He told Genoveve as much when she questioned his long silences.

"Aw, pffftt," Genoveve said, and mimed tossing a handful of that to the birds. "Just say it, whatever you got. I'm saving all my getting pissed for the next world."

She motioned at the sky. Denny looked surprised.

"Heaven," he said carefully. "Is that what you mean?"

Genoveve's eyes narrowed. "Course. What's gonna jerk my chain more than a bunch of angels?"

Denny said, "You don't seem the type, that's all. To believe."

"Hmmm." Genoveve streamed smoke and squinted at him. "You got doubts."

"Doubts?"

She pointed to his eyes. "I see 'em. You're the heaven sort yourself, but you ain't too sure, are ya."

After a moment, Denny said, "I sometimes wonder if we're wrong. And there's nothing after this life at all."

"Sometimes?"

"Now and then."

Genoveve swept her hand at their surroundings. "Now?"

Denny considered. "Not right now."

"Good." Genoveve filled her hand with Cool Whip. "Because I'm thinking, 'If he don't believe in heaven, what's he doing here?' This would be no way to spend your one and only time around.'"

They were silent, contemplating the yard.

"I'll take some more refreshment," Denny said, and motioned for Cool Whip.

All the while, the dog was barking.

Denny and Genoveve pooled intelligence, and began to eliminate neighbors. It couldn't be the divorced one with the Bush-Cheney stickers still in his car window – he had no yard and the acoustics of the bark said outdoors. It couldn't be the Mormon couple who worked out by stalking around with ski poles – they were the self-appointed noise police of this block. That left the creepy kid who always wore Band Aids and was fresh out of jail or college (rumors were 50:50 on that score). He seemed to be alone in his place.

Through a crack Genoveve widened in the boards across her windows, she and Denny saw chew toys and garbage bags in the corner of the kid's yard, ravaged like a dog had raided them. The rest of the yard was out of sight, but, yep, the kid was looking like their culprit.

To Denny, the kid's age changed the game entirely. No one under twenty-five could be reasoned with. That demographic was motivated only by brands or followers (which, Denny explained, were gained by publishing everything but your nail clippings on the Internet). Two squinting seniors, one of them dressed like a trailer-park faith healer, were not exactly going to strike this kid as a worthy brand or follower.

Well then, Genoveve announced, they were going on an adventure. She'd dress up, and Denny down. They'd take the young fellow some mayo cake, and something for the dog too. They'd say: how about it, kid, can we work something out here.

They met later that day, outside the kid's gate. Genoveve had spent two hours getting ready, and now she looked like a movie star, back when they knew how to make them. In that one-way trip to Hollywood all those years ago, Genoveve had gotten nothing but a bunch of stolen costumes. She knew they'd come in handy someday.

For the first time in years, Denny felt the here and now. As he held the gate open for Genoveve, he noticed plane trails in the sky shaped like an exclamation mark. The two of them laughed at this unfortunate omen.

"Now remember," Genoveve said, "Don't look at him like we done know him already. Look at him like we're ready to learn."

"I can do that," Denny said.

They set off together toward the kid's door, in the buttery August sun.

ESSAY

THANKSGIVING 2020

Memo

The year 2020 has been... well, you know. You were there.

The experience of this year has, I think, been less monolithic than popularly acknowledged. ("Honestly?" a friend said to me when we chanced on each other in the street. "It's been wonderful. I've seen my kids—I mean, really seen them—and remembered things I didn't know I'd forgotten. You're the first person I've said that out loud to, though. To bliss out in a pandemic seems, you know...") Some people have been exiled from their happiest selves by the pandemic; others have been reunited with them. All of these personal struggles or growths have played out amid a global crush of untimely death that has made many of us defensive or sheepish about being happy or unhappy. We're still alive, after all. What is surely true for everyone, though, is that this year has had impact. It's hard to imagine a person who has not been changed in some way by the brute force of collective standstill.

I hear talk of "life getting back to normal after the vaccine". Out of respect for the general frailty of hope right now, I nod along and swallow my comeback. Normal life, I might otherwise say, is always as cruel and capricious as this virus. Planes drop out of the sky, indifferent to the love stories and intellectual breakthroughs and parental hopes thereby stunted. The good guy gets cancer, the bad guy gets the condo. A lifetime's work is lost in the fire, but a baby sock is spared.

That's life as it really is. But we have the luxury—in the developed world, at least—of forgetting it most of the time. We blueprint dreams onto days not yet lived and then rely on them like maps, even though they are as instantly collapsible as cobwebs. We use strident possessives like *my* wife and *my* son, as though other people are not merely lent to us on terms we won't know until they are revoked. We know nothing, and own nothing, and because that is existentially untenable, we use story-telling to build purpose, create territory, and adopt rhythm and register in our feelings. And in so doing, we have some of the greatest experiences possible as a human being. We love, we protect, we devise. The absurdity of thinking the future is obedient to us is more than offset by the glory of the things we do to convince ourselves it's true.

To me, the pandemic has been an affirmation of both of those things equally: the absurdity and the glory. If it's ridiculous to plan to propose under a particular peach tree in Crete on winter solstice, when the potential spouse or the money or the tree might be gone by then, it's even more ridiculous *not* to. The art of it, I figure, is to be flexible on the specifics. So it might become a proposal under parking lot lamplight, with what belongings we grabbed, before the wild fire arrived, crushed up against the backseat window. I will accept that as the rewrite life handed back of the storyline I submitted. I will not resent the shortfall because the perfect version was never real anyway. Life isn't our flawless projections of it. In being less than that, it is so much more.

I have done almost none of what I had hoped to do this year. I have done instead things that would have looked like jackass doodles in my original plans for 2020. I have painstakingly annotated flight manuals in baby steps toward my pilot's license. I have learned how to dead-lift. I have realized how much better my life is when I hear my mother's voice every day. I have reconnected with Paris, where I happily drifted as a teenager. I have read scores of Pulitzer-Prize-winning novels and remembered that the written word is the highest calling, at least to me. I have created, but not what I thought I would. (In what might explain why I am particularly mindful of the intention-outcome gap in life, that often happens in creating, though.)

I don't regret a thing. I don't want you to, either.

Which brings me to...

Laughter cannot be caged

Before I came upon *A Brief For The Defense* by Jack Gilbert, I would struggle to name "my favorite poem". I had many favorite lines, clipped from this poem and that. But an overall poem - just one, that I would choose if I could carry only a single poem in my head for the rest of my life - no, not really. I used to say William Ernest Henley's *Invictus* because it's the Rage Against The Machine of poetry. But it wasn't until Jack Gilbert, a poet I encountered only in my thirties, that I had my real answer.

If you have not yet read Jack Gilbert's *A Brief For The Defense*, here's where to pause in reading me and go read him instead.

You will see that Gilbert's poem opens with sorrow, slaughter and starving babies. He packs all of those things into his first three lines, noting that they are ubiquitous and inevitable. In other words: this ain't the way to Disneyland, folks.

The poem maintains this grim view throughout: the world we must witness, if we are alive at all, is fucking *awful*. It just is. But I'm no disciple of misery and this view alone is not the reason I love the poem. It is the other reality that Gilbert sets alongside the first: laughter, and by extension joy, is everywhere too, even in the bleakest of places.

As Gilbert observes in his poem, laughter cannot be caged. Laughter doesn't confine itself to places of plenty or of freedom. It doesn't wait for the sun to come up, or for rescue to arrive. Every day, people find ways to be happy, on the weakest of premises, just as plants will find the faintest hint of light and bend toward it. And by doing this—Gilbert calls it to "risk delight"—we properly honor the suffering in the world. To not be happy whenever and however we can is, in fact, to become an accomplice in and champion of suffering. The most noble response to the cruelty of life is to reject the idea that it makes joy impossible. The reality is, it is our nature to be joyful anyhow. That nature might be callous if weighed intellectually, but viscerally it is the truth.

For a long time, I've wanted to write something in the vein of

Gilbert's poem. I suppose I've never found myself in the ropes of suffering quite enough to access the best words about it. Like everyone else, I've had my low points, but I'm a first-world white chick with a thorough education and a doggedly supportive family. Sorrow and slaughter haven't come and scraped at my door; they have only been hologrammed into my living room as news reports and movie plotlines. War is a video game. Starvation is an eating disorder. Wounds are foremost of the heart, and waiting room magazines have answers for them. What do I really know about suffering?

And then 2020 happened.

Gratitude in the time of Covid

This year, I wanted my Thanksgiving message to center on continuation.

To be clear, I have not lost anyone to the coronavirus, or suffered very much more, on the scale of things, than inconvenience. I hope the same is true for you. But the Johns Hopkins death maps on which countries across the world turn red, then orange, then red again, like malfunctioning stoplights, sent me back to Jack Gilbert. To paraphrase him, if patients are not dying someplace, they are dying somewhere else. For once, we cannot simply turn off the TV and forget the ubiquity of suffering, because our fear of it is imprinted on our every lived moment: the grandkids who can't visit, the smiles unseen behind masks, the six-feet reminders and the store admittance lanes that after a while make our bodies feel as dangerous as butcher knives.

In a first for my generation, the future has asked for collective forbearance. I don't think my generation has the tools for this, I said to my mother as the pandemic stretched on into summer. We're productivity, energy drinks, same-day delivery, and pioneers of a form of "following" that doesn't involve actual movement. We're low-tolerance go-getters. Sacrifice and holding still are not necessarily things we know how to do.

It remains to be seen if my generation will endure standstill less gracefully than older generations. We can only review how we did once it's over. The W.H.O. recently warned that young low-risk people likely will not get the vaccine until year 2022. If that timeline proves accurate, we are only one third of the way done. One third. And that assumes vaccination is a silver bullet. Forgive me, but the only silver bullet I believe in is a quarter dropping into a jukebox.

Coping stratagems, then—sturdy ones that span months, not weeks—seem like a good idea at this point. This year's Thanksgiving poem captures one of the comforts I found in Paris this summer: nature, and the way it keeps on going about its business, and the tendency of people to keep on going about their business too, even in the worst of circumstances.

Thanksgiving poem 2020

The poem I wrote for Thanksgiving 2020, with all of the above thoughts in my head, is overleaf.

Photograph overleaf: Wall art in Paris, captured October 2022 by Zoe Marie Bel.

Memo (Still)   *Thanksgiving poem 2020*

Over the rooftops, piano scales, hobbling.
A tough year, say headlines and the
Lines on faces, everything suspended.
But, still, these spilled paints of sundown.
The gusts at the head of the towpath,
The linen strung high between leaning walls.
The porches where still the love-worn watch
Courtyard shadows slowly turning.
Still the scudding clouds and the thing said
Aloud after many world-spins of yearning.

Still apocalyptic teen lovers scrape 'Forever'
Into bark that would eye-roll if it could.
Still the athletic-wear moms tap off ash
As their kids scuff gravel at pigeons.
Still no heroes and all heroes. Still bastards
Dying in river-rescues of dogs, while the
War-medaled freeze at phantom threats and
The next generation reviews the old one in
Spray paint. Still the midnight thud of street ball:
The home-broken remembering they're children.

Yes, there is anguish, the great undone.
But the vermillion loiter of sun in the cracks
Of the city reminds us: suffering has never won.
The casual magnificence with which the world
Is dappled didn't get the memo about pain.
Because, all the same, the stillborn raindrops on
The window hold the last light of day, and
The river barge dips its ropes as it sways.

Final thoughts at Thanksgiving 2020

In the Place des Vosges in August, I watched a toddler blow soap bubbles into the air, bubbles that flurried and flounced into the six-feet radii around passers-by as irrepressibly as, well, laughter. Heads turned, and dogs were set barking or capering after the transparent invaders, until they vaporized on the sidewalk or were stamped out by other children.

I think about that moment a lot now. The "Capital-B Big" moments in life—graduation, promotion, or marriage, for example—may be subject to last-minute changes in the year to come. Some people, I understand, will feel cheated or demoralized as it becomes clear our hopes for the future were never promises from it. But small moments like a bubble outbreak in a park won't ever stop, just as a cage won't ever keep out laughter.

Maybe the coming months are a chance not to miss out on those small things, for once.

Zoe Marie Bel, Paris, December 2020

There isn't time, so brief is life, for bickerings, apologies, heartburnings, callings to account. There is only time for loving, and but an instant, so to speak, for that.

–Mark Twain

Compass

When the words don't line up like they should,
And the gridlock won't ease, or the shortcut make good;
When the apology is weak, but the profit bold,
And the doubts creak on and the barkeep scolds;
When the blossom is rain-felled, the old photo lost,
The dollars inadequate, the steps over-mossed;
When the grand plan is now archived in daydreams,
And a letter says goodbye, leaves the future unseamed;
I just walk by a light that is mine and no other:
I walk toward the ways of my mother.

With all my love, mum

Acknowledgements

Short story *Care* was first published by *Short Édition*.

If I tried to thank everyone who has encouraged me in my work over the years, this book would be the size of a brick and about as entertaining to behold as one. I will instead endeavor to thank each of you personally in my own way, so hang in there *and* on to your hats, if that's not too much hanging to take on all at once.

Particular thanks are owed to Bay Backner, Jaimie Kourt and her family, and Hannah Croft, all of whom have been patient and judicious readers of draft after draft of many of the pieces here. I am also especially grateful to John Fuller, who was briefly my tutor, then has guided and inspired my growth immeasurably ever since, as my friend. John's own poem *Valentine* is one of my lifelong favorites.

And of course: thank you to Maggie, Roy, Sio and Davey, Jamie and Rebecca, Elliot and Jo, and Roberta, and all the children they've conjured up between them: Betsy, Arwen, Lucy, Atticus, Ted, Daphne, and Elizabeth. These folks have fed me, given me creative space, forgiven me time and time again for missed birthdays, and never once called me a jerk for not giving up.

INDEX

About the author

Zoe Marie Bel writes fiction and poetry. Her debut short story collection *Hard Place Rock* and her debut novel *After The Angels* are forthcoming. A number of poems in this slimbook also appear in full-length collection *Passengers*, which Zoe expects to finish in 2024. She was born in England, but that wasn't her fault. She now bounces around the world a great deal, and in particular between Los Angeles and Paris. Find out more about her work, read online pieces and follow news at ZoeMarieBel.com.